A Special F

Written by Adam and Charlotte Guillain

Tess and Finn were waving their mum off to work. It was Saturday, but she sometimes had to work at the wildlife park at weekends. As her mum left, Tess turned to her dad and said, "At least we get to play with you!"

Dad ruffled Tess's hair and sighed. "I'm really sorry, but I have to take Dylan to a party this morning," he said. "I've arranged for you and Finn to play at Rav's flat."

"Okay," said Finn, but he wished he could spend the day with his dad.

After Dad had dropped them off at Rav's flat, Finn started
to grumble.

"We never get to see our mum and dad. They're always too
busy," he muttered.

Mrs Joshi put her arm around his shoulders.

"You know that they work very hard," she said.

"That's why they're so tired all the time," said Tess with a frown.

"Maybe we could make a nice surprise for them?" suggested Mrs Joshi.

Tess's face lit up. "Yes please!" she cried.

What sort of surprise?

Mrs Joshi smiled. "Well, your mum is at work all day and your dad said he's going to see your grandparents this afternoon. Who is going to cook for you all this evening?"

Tess and Finn looked at each other and shrugged.

"We are!" Mrs Joshi said, laughing. "We can make them a special dinner!"

Tess, Finn and Rav cheered.

"That's a brilliant idea, Mum!" cried Rav.

"What can we make?" Tess wondered.

"Let's plan the menu," said Mrs Joshi.

Rav fetched some paper and pencils.

Soon they were sitting around the kitchen table.

"Now, what do your mum and dad like to eat?" asked Mrs Joshi.

"Dad likes burgers," said Tess.

"Mum doesn't eat meat!" said Finn.

"Dad likes spicy food," said Tess.

"I don't!" said Finn.

They spent the next hour writing down a list of ideas and crossing things off it. At last, Tess held up a piece of paper with the menu they'd agreed on.

"Wait," said Finn, the smile fading from his face. "Where will we get all the ingredients from?"

Mrs Joshi smiled. "Your dad told me there's all sorts of things growing in your garden downstairs," she said.

"Of course!" gasped Tess.

They ran out of the flat and downstairs into Tess and Finn's garden.

"There are so many ripe tomatoes," said Finn, starting to pick them. "Perfect for the chutney!"

"We can use these carrots, courgettes and peppers in the curry," said Tess.

"There aren't any apples for the crumble," said Rav, looking around.

"Don't worry, I've got some apples," said his mum. "But I know something we can add to them." She led them out of the gate, towards the play area.

"Blackberries!" cried Finn.

They carefully picked the juicy berries from the bramble bush.

"My fingers are purple!" said Tess, holding up her hands.

"Right, I think we've got everything we need now," said
Mrs Joshi. "Let's go and start cooking!"

Back in the flat, they got to work. When the chutney was made and the curry was bubbling on the cooker, delicious smells started to fill the flat.

"I'm hungry!" said Rav.

"Time to stop and make lunch," said his mum, giving the chutney a final stir.

As they munched their sandwiches, they made more plans.

"I'll write up the menu in my best handwriting," said Tess.

"I could put our names on cards so we know where to sit," suggested Finn.

"Your parents will love it!" said Rav.

I hope so!

By the time they had made the crumble and washed up, the three friends were exhausted.

"Do you want to watch a film until your dad comes to take you home?" said Rav, flopping down on the sofa.

"Yes please," said Finn, collapsing beside him.

Ding dong! The doorbell made them jump. Mrs Joshi went to open it and Dylan ran in, followed by Tess and Finn's dad.

"Come on, kids," he said with a grin. "I've just ordered a takeaway for our tea!"

Tess and Finn stopped and stared.

"What are we going to do?" Mrs Joshi whispered as Tess put on her coat.

"I don't know," Tess whispered back, "but we'll try to think of something! Thank you for having us!" she added loudly.

"Yes, thanks!" called Finn.

Back at home, Tess and Finn tried to work out a plan.

"We're going to have so much food," groaned Tess.

"It'll be enough for the whole of Comet Street!" said Finn.

An idea popped into Tess's head. "Exactly! Great idea, Finn!"

Huh?

"Can you ask Mrs Joshi to bring down the food?" said Tess. "I've got to do something else."

"Okay," said Finn, and he went to Rav's flat.

"How are you going to eat this *and* a takeaway?" Rav asked Finn as they carried the food down.

Finn shrugged. "I don't know!" he said.

He was surprised to see Asha and her dad carrying chairs outside.

"Wait for us!" called Stefan, while his mum and sister carried a table out into the hallway.

Finn's mum opened the door and stared at everyone in astonishment.

"You're not the delivery man!" she said.

"We cooked dinner for you and Dad," Finn explained.

Just then the takeaway arrived.

"Oh no!" gasped his mum.

"We've got too much food," said Tess in the hallway, "but not if everyone eats it. Let's take some chairs outside to the garden!"

Her mum's face flipped from a frown to a smile and she started to laugh. "Great idea!" she said.

Let's eat this special feast!

Talk about the story

Answer the questions:

1 Where did Tess and Finn's mum work at the weekends?

2 What sort of food did Tess say that her dad liked?

3 What does the word 'fading' mean (page 10)?
   Can you use it in another sentence?

4 What vegetables were the friends going to use in the curry?

5 Why did they have to be careful about picking
   the blackberries?

6 Why did Tess ask the neighbours to share their food?

7 Describe how you think Tess and Finn's parents felt when
   they found out that the friends had made them dinner.

8 If you were making a meal for your friends or family, what
   would you cook? Who would you invite?

Can you retell the story in your own words?